P-51
p. 69

WRIGHT ON!

A Collection of Political Cartoons

by DON WRIGHT

SIMON AND SCHUSTER · New York

To Carolyn and the preservation of opinion

WAR

WAR, says Youth, isn't so much hell as it is outmoded.

Youth demonstrates, riots, gets high, cops out, pleads, bleeds, rages, begs and goes to Canada. Big Government cranks a heavy, bureaucratic metal ear in their direction and the illusion is one of listening and hearing—until their number comes up and it orders them to arms in the name of patriotism. Then they are pointed across the sea to mortar, bombs, bullets, napalm and shredded humanity.

Youth is involved and restless, putting it mildly; frustrated and tormented, putting it truthfully. Painful questions put to their parents and their government go unanswered.

So, in the cartoons ahead you'll find commentary on war. The war cartoons are dedicated to Youth. They do the fighting and dying and they are the only hope for an end to fighting and dying.

GEN. THIEU

WANTS **YOU**

2/14/68

11/7/69

THE SILENT MAJORITY

"IT'S JOHN WAYNE! I KNEW HE'D COME!"

8/13/69

August 6, 1969: Eight Green Berets, including the com-mander of the U.S. Army Special Forces in Vietnam, were charged with the June 20, 1969, torture and murder of Thai Khac Chuyen, a Vietnamese double agent. The men were held under guard in small, dank cells at the sprawling Long Binh Army base 12 miles north of Saigon.

Not long before this incident, some of the American movie-going public watched John Wayne amble through the jungles of Vietnam thrashing the Communists with make-believe bullets and generally glorifying the effectiveness of this elite corps of jungle fighters. The movie was titled, ring-ingly, The Green Berets.

8/20/69

Thai Khac Chuyen, the slain double agent, worked as an interpreter for the Green Berets and belonged to an intelligence ring funded by the Central Intelligence Agency. It was the CIA which suggested that the Berets "get rid of" him.

10/1/69

The U.S. Army, after refusing comment on the charges that
eight of its Green Berets drugged Chuyen, shot him, wrapped
him in chains and threw him into the South China Sea, finally
decided to drop prosecution of the case after the CIA refused
to provide witnesses "in the interest of national security."

11/20/69

November 24, 1969: The Army ordered a "life or death" court-martial for 1st Lieutenant William L. Calley, Jr., on charges of murdering 109 South Vietnamese civilians on March 16, 1968, in the village of My Lai 4.

DARK AT THE TOP OF THE STAIRS 12/12/69

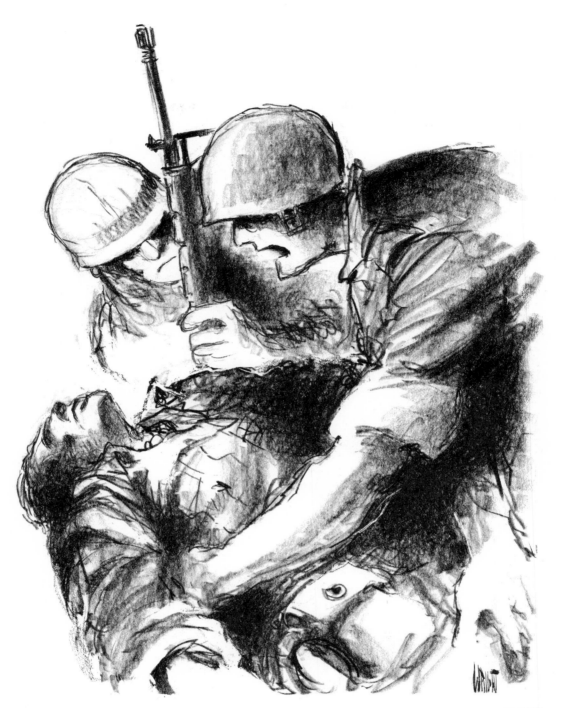

"I WAS JUST GOING TO TELL HIM THEY'RE GETTING SERIOUS IN PARIS."

11/1/68

October 31, 1968: In a dramatic television broadcast from the White House, President Lyndon B. Johnson ordered a halt to all bombing of North Vietnam beginning at 8 A.M. the next day. Because of this move, the President said he had reason to believe the North Vietnamese would begin "prompt, productive, serious and intensive negotiations" at the Paris peace talks being conducted by the U.S., South Vietnam, North Vietnam and the National Liberation Front.

16

10/31/67

"NOBODY WON THE NOBEL PEACE PRIZE!"

In 1966 and 1967 there was very little peace in the world and no real candidate for the Nobel Peace Prize. Martin Luther King, Jr., won it in 1964, the United Nation's Children's Emergency Fund, in 1965. But it was not given again until Professor René Cassin, principal author of the United Nations Declaration of the Rights of Man, won it in 1968.

"YOU MEAN YOU WERE BLUFFING?"

7/7/65

1/7/70   "FILCHED FIVE GUNBOATS FROM FRANCE, SWIPED ONE OF OUR RADAR
INSTALLATIONS—PRAISE ALLAH, WHAT NEXT?"

"FASTEST GUN IN THE MIDEAST."   11/12/68

20

9/11/69 "ONCE AGAIN THE COWARDLY ISRAELIS ATTEMPTED A RAID INSIDE EGYPTIAN
TERRITORY. OUR FORCES SHOT DOWN SIX ISRAELI JETS, DESTROYED
40 ISRAELI TANKS AND KILLED 750 ISRAELI SOLDIERS."

"IS THAT YOUR FINAL REPLY, MRS. MEIR?" 12/24/69

TECHNOLOGY

8/19/68

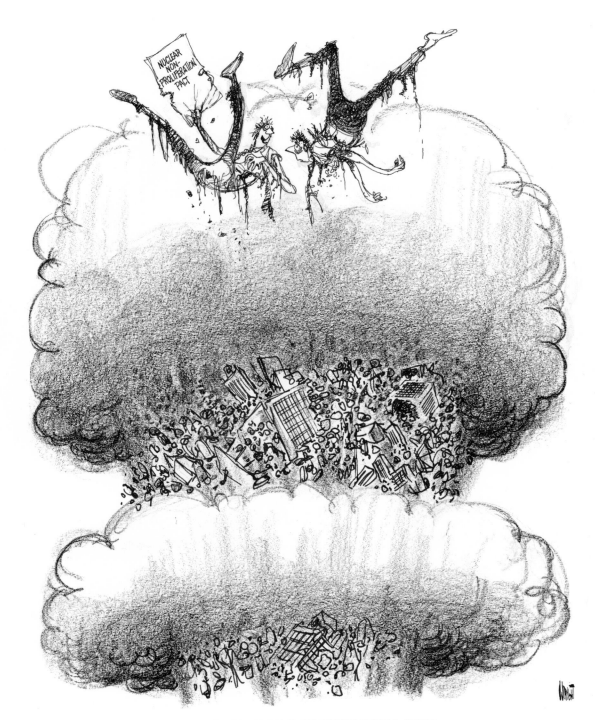

11/25/69

"YOU'LL BE PLEASED TO KNOW IT WAS NONE
OF US TREATY SIGNERS."

"IT MUST BE HELL IN NORTHERN IRELAND."

5/2/69

Northern Ireland, plagued with riots, strikes, sabotage and explosions since October 1968, was the scene of civil rights disorders between the Unionist Party Protestants and the Nationalist Party Roman Catholics. The Catholics, who are outnumbered two to one by the Protestants, claimed they were discriminated against in jobs, housing and voting.

5/25/69

"SORRY, FATHER—FROM THE BACK YOU LOOKED LIKE A PROTESTANT."

3/29/68

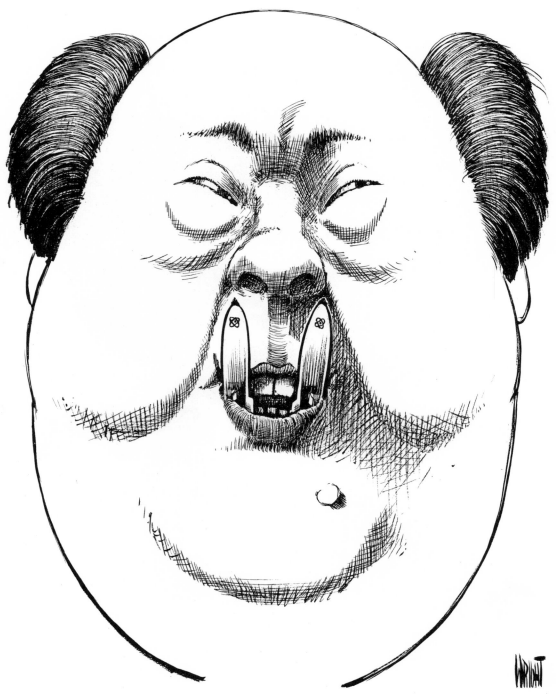

3/12/66

10/2/69

1/7/68

Dean Rusk on the Vietnam war.

29

3/13/68

March 11, 1968: Senate Foreign Relations Committee Chairman J. William Fulbright thought he had Secretary of State Dean Rusk right where he wanted him—testifying before the Committee and the nation on the Administration's Vietnam war policy. But in two days of televised testimony, Fulbright failed to pin Rusk down on anything, and the match ended in a stalemate.

8/18/69

"—IT WILL BE YOUR JOB, MR. NIXON, TO END THE WAR EVEN
THOUGH THE ENEMY IS STEPPING UP THE FIGHT AND
REFUSES TO NEGOTIATE HONESTLY. SHOULD YOU OR YOUR
IRON FORCE FAIL, WE WILL DENY ALL KNOWLEDGE
OF YOUR EXISTENCE IN 1972 . . ."

31

3/26/69

9/24/69

September 19, 1969: President Nixon canceled draft calls for a total of 50,000 men for the remainder of the year. He also announced plans for draft reform by executive order if Congress failed to act on his draft proposals.

"YOU WON A LOTTERY—WHAT'S THE PRIZE?"

12/2/69

December 1, 1969: The first draft lottery in recent times was conducted. President Nixon, after asking for and receiving authorization from Congress in the fall, instituted the system under which the priority for calling young men to military service would be determined by the order in which their birth dates were drawn at random from a fishbowl.

34

2/8/67   **"WE FINALLY FOUND A USE FOR IT."**

"IN CAMBODIA WE KNOW WHAT TO DO WITH AMERICAN WEAPONS."

4/21/70

April 1970: The U.S. agreed to supply arms to the newly established military government of Cambodia which had deposed neutralist head of state Prince Norodom Sihanouk. The agreement came at a time when the new government was whipping up a campaign against 600,000 Vietnamese who lived in Cambodia, and wholesale massacres of Vietnamese civilians began to occur.

36

5/1/70   **"WELL, NIXON WAS THE ONE."**

April 30, 1970: In a stunning turn of policy, President Nixon announced on nationwide television that he was escalating the war in Indochina by launching a surprise offensive by U.S. and South Vietnamese troops against North Vietnamese and Viet Cong "sanctuaries" in Cambodia.

1/29/68

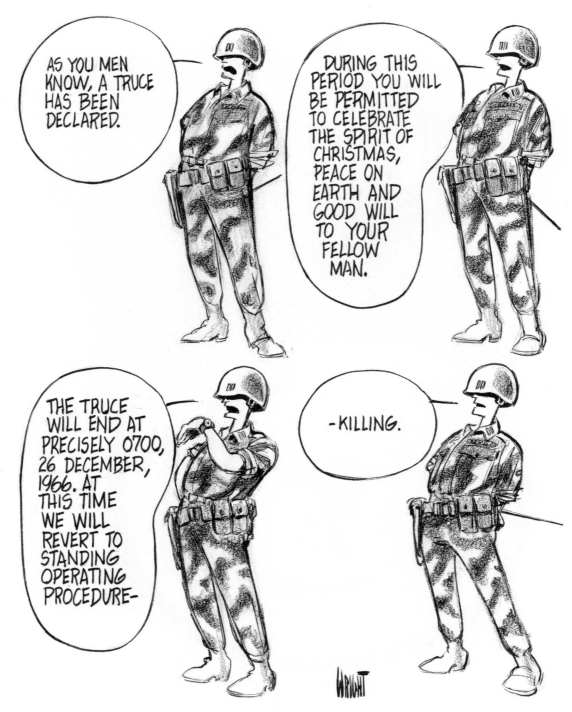

38

12/23/66

"MAY I TAKE THIS OPPORTUNITY TO WISH YOU AND YOURS
A VERY HAPPY AND PROSPEROUS NEW YEAR."

1/1/70

1/13/70

THE VANQUISHED

The Biafran War of Secession, after 31 months of fighting
and two million deaths from starvation, ended in January
1970, when the tiny rebel nation collapsed and three to five
million Ibo tribesmen were left to their fate. It had begun
May 30, 1967, because of tribal animosities between the
Yorubas in the west, the Moslem Hausas in the north and the
sophisticated Christian Ibos in the east.

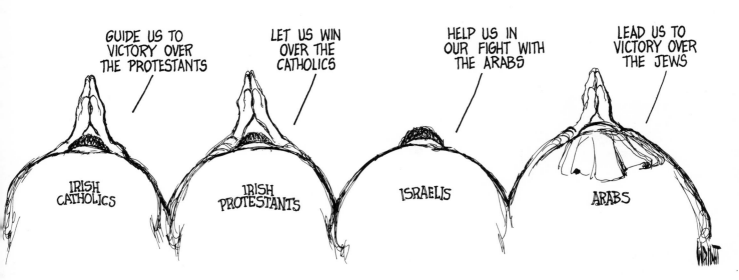

GUIDE US TO VICTORY OVER THE PROTESTANTS

LET US WIN OVER THE CATHOLICS

HELP US IN OUR FIGHT WITH THE ARABS

LEAD US TO VICTORY OVER THE JEWS

IRISH CATHOLICS

IRISH PROTESTANTS

ISRAELIS

ARABS

8/27/69

THE NATION

To TRY and isolate problems at home from problems elsewhere is deceiving. The world is one with our problems now. Technology has made it so.

Pollution, poverty, riots, equality and violence are not problems exclusive to the good old U.S.A. It's just that here in an open society our cuts are bleeding in front of a packed house.

It must be clear to the rest of the world that if the United States fails to cope with these problems, there is little hope that any civilization can. We all might "progress" ourselves right out of business.

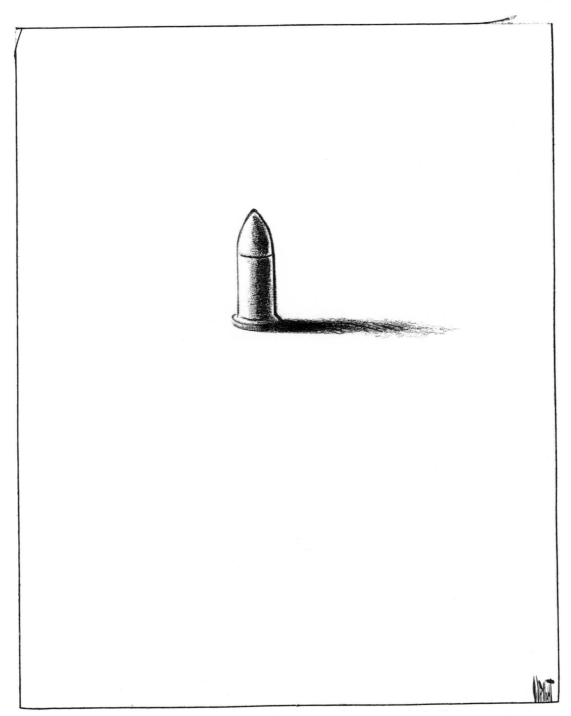

AS AMERICAN AS APPLE PIE 6/6/68

In the early morning of June 5th, 1968, just after winning the California Democratic primary, Senator Robert F. Kennedy was shot at the Ambassador Hotel in Los Angeles by Sirhan Sirhan, and he died on June 6th, 1968, from the wound.

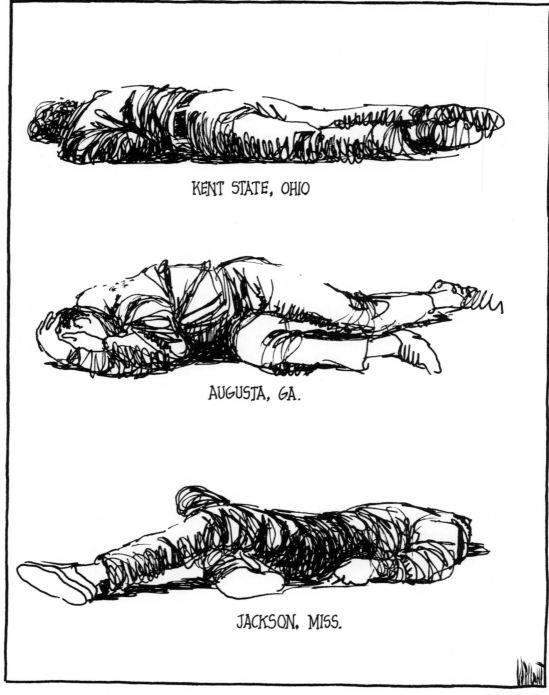

KENT STATE, OHIO

AUGUSTA, GA.

JACKSON, MISS.

5/18/70

LAW AND ORDER

May 4, 1970: Four students, two male, two female, were shot to death by Ohio National Guardsmen during an antiwar demonstration at Kent State University.

May 11, 1970: Six Negro men were shot to death during a riot in Augusta, Georgia. The police admitted to shooting five of them in the back, while the sixth died of gunshot wounds of undetermined origin. The county medical examiner's report revealed that one of the five men had been shot nine times.

May 15, 1970: Two students were shot to death in Jackson, Mississippi, when police opened fire on a group of Negro men standing in front of a women's dormitory at the predominantly black Jackson State College.

1/5/70

12/18/69

"HUMANS ARE FILTHY"

12/26/69

"O BEAUTIFUL FOR SPACIOUS SKIES, FOR AMBER WAVES OF GRAIN,
FOR PURPLE MOUNTAIN MAJESTIES, ABOVE THE . . ."

2/14/69

6/12/68

5/8/69

May 7, 1969: The Pentagon announced tentative plans to ship, via rail to the East Coast, large amounts of obsolete or unserviceable chemical agents—including deadly nerve gas—for disposal in the Atlantic Ocean. Most of the 27,000 tons of material would come from the Rocky Mountain Arsenal near Denver and the Edgewood Arsenal in Maryland.

September 9, 1969: After 2,500 cylinders of lethal gas had already been shipped, the U.S. Department of Transportation announced that because of public outcry it was canceling further shipments from the Denver arsenal.

6/5/69   "OOPS"

"OKAY, FUN'S OVER."   11/27/69

November 25, 1969: President Nixon renounced the use of biological weapons and declared the U.S. would never be the first to use lethal chemical weapons. On February 14, he took it a step further and announced he was banning military use of disease-producing toxins and directed the destruction of existing toxin stockpiles.

54

3/24/70

March 1970: In defiance of Federal law, the nation's first postal strike spread rapidly through four states, diverting tens of millions of pieces of mail and prompting President Nixon to call out regular troops and National Guardsmen to move the mail in New York City. Postal workers were demanding a long-overdue pay raise.

3/20/70

4/1/70

That same month the air traffic controllers also went on strike, causing flight delays, monumental air traffic jams and inadequately staffed control towers at major airports throughout the nation. The controllers wanted better working conditions, better equipment, less overtime and higher pay. They claimed a combination of air traffic, fatigue and obsolete equipment was endangering safety of air traffic control system.

8/3/67

7/4/69

July 3, 1969: The Nixon Administration issued its long-awaited statement on school desegregation. It was acknowledged, in political circles, as a significant concession to the segregationist South.

9/1/69

September 1969: Sixty-five of the U.S. Justice Department's seventy-two civil rights lawyers signed a petition protesting what they termed a relaxation of the government's desegregation enforcement.

In October of 1969 the U.S. Supreme Court tossed out the 15-year-old desegregation doctrine of "all deliberate speed," saying that it no longer is "constitutionally permissible." It directed the Fifth U.S. Circuit Court of Appeals to implement its orders, and the appellate court set December 31, 1969, as the deadline for a "unitary" school system in Mississippi. The ruling, which wiped out the "freedom of choice" system which brought only token integration, affected 33 of Mississippi's 149 school districts. In response to the order Governor John Bell Williams called for a statewide private school system. These schools were hurriedly set up in most of the 33 districts, and a mass movement of whites from public to private schools began.

"HELLO! HELLOOOOOO—HELLOOOOOO—
HELLOOOOOO . . ."   1/6/70

SOUTHERN SCHOOL DESEGREGATION

SUPREME COURT

MITCHELL

11/13/69

12/22/69

...MORE
CIVIL RIGHTS
LEGISLATION
THAN ANY
OTHER
PRESIDENT

WRIGHT

4/9/68

NON-VIOLENCE

4/1/68

March 28, 1968: Six days prior to his assassination on April 4, at the Lorraine Motel in Memphis, Tennessee, Dr. Martin Luther King's nonviolent march in support of striking city garbage collectors turned into a bloody street battle which left one dead, 37 wounded and 105 arrested. The violence began when several hundred Negro youths suddenly bolted out of the 3,000-man march and began roaming through the streets on a burning and pillaging rampage.

"GO BACK TO YOUR HOMES AND ACT LIKE
CIVILIZED HUMAN BEINGS."

3/14/68

64

4/12/68

"WHAT'S INDIVISIBLE MEAN?"

"THAT SETTLES IT—SEVEN TO SIX AGAINST
CIVIL DISOBEDIENCE."

12/9/69

9/29/69

"PERSONALLY, I THINK KIDS LEARN A LOT
WATCHING TV."

"SEE ME CLOBBER THAT COP?"

2/12/68

68

5/7/68

"IT ALL BEGAN WHEN THOSE WITH MUCH TO LEARN TOOK OVER FROM THOSE WITH MUCH TO TEACH."

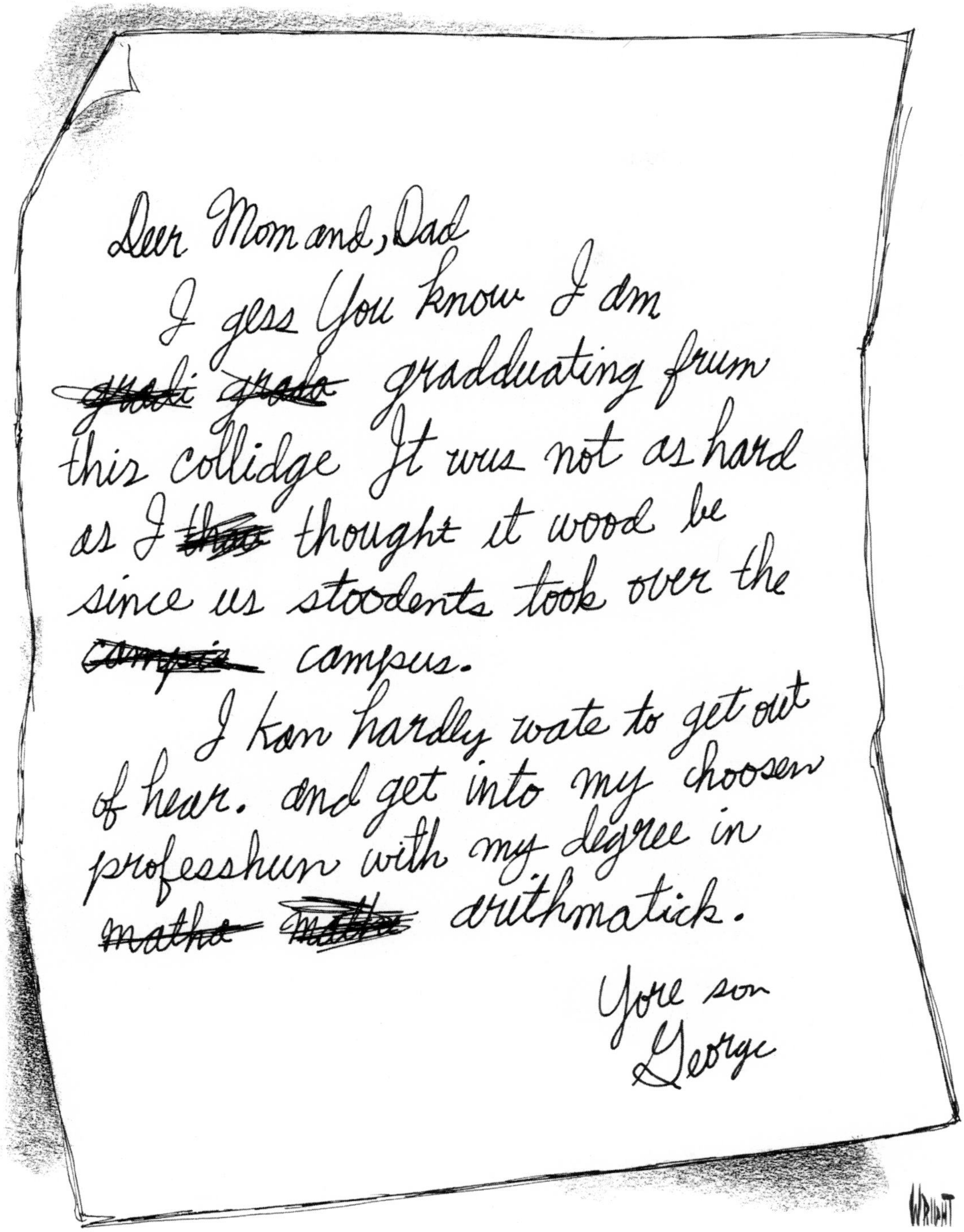

Deer Mom and, Dad

I gess You know I am ~~gudi grade~~ gradduating frum this collidge It wus not as hard as I ~~thot~~ thought it wood be since us stoodents took over the ~~campus~~ campsus.

I kan hardly wate to get out of hear. and get into my choosen professhun with my degree in ~~maths~~ ~~maths~~ arithmatick.

Yore son
George

WRIGHT

1/29/69

4/8/67

"HE'S GONE JOE COLLEGE ON US."

During the first six months of 1967 the young set was turned on by the Mellow Yellow craze. Discovered by a hippie newspaper in Berkeley, California, and predicted by Donovan, the British folksinger, "Mellow Yellow" was a description of the high acquired from smoking the inside of the banana's yellow peel. To acquire the finished product, called bananadrine, the peel had to be scraped, roasted in an oven and crushed in a blender. The peel was said to contain sero tonim, an agent that can cause distortion of the mental processes.

"I SAY CENSOR BOOKS, CENSOR PICTURES AND CENSOR
SEX EDUCATION SO THAT KIDS GROW UP
TO BE LIKE US ADULTS."

12/29/69

3/11/70   "IF YOU'VE DONE NOTHING WRONG, YOU HAVE NOTHING TO FEAR—
THIS IS STILL THE UNITED STATES OF AMERICA. YOU
WERE BROUGHT HERE SIMPLY BECAUSE YOU
JUST DON'T LOOK RIGHT TO US."

"ONE OF THOSE RADICALS WITH A BEARD AND LONG HAIR."

4/4/69

Easter 1969

THE OFFICEHOLDERS

CYNICAL SOCIETY. We can no longer entrust to it the random use of the word "politician," since hardly anybody can say it without sneering.

Some argue that the editorial cartoonist is partly responsible. He (and why aren't there any she's in this business?) transforms an elected idol into a babbling mortal, tarnished and naked, with human frailties. What's left is a politician.

But it is possible, the electorate believes, for some men to indulge in politics and remain a cut above being called a politician. (When a politician's politician retires, he becomes a "statesman.")

The following cartoons then, to be fair, comment on some of the more illuminating officeholders of our times—such as illuminating officeholder Johnson, illuminating officeholder Nixon, illuminating officeholder Romney. And Spiro Agnew.

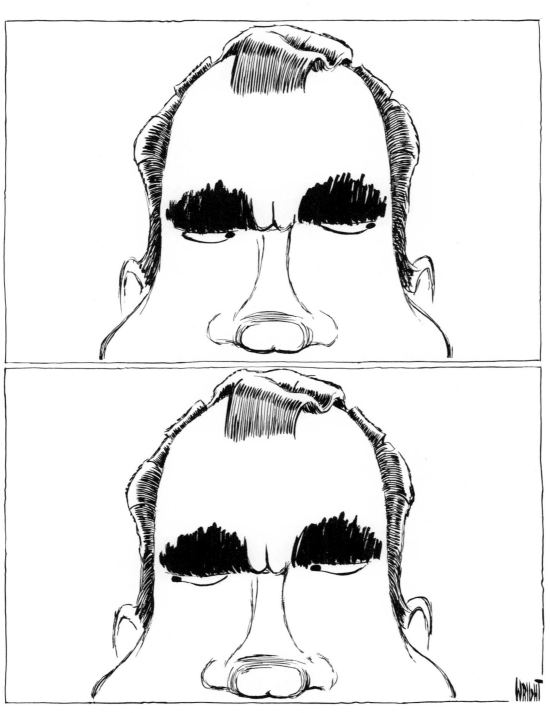

78

11/11/68   "WHY DOES EVERYBODY DO THAT WHEN I INTRODUCE YOU AS THE
NEXT VICE-PRESIDENT OF THE UNITED STATES?"

"THE PRESIDENT WANTS HIM TAKEN FOR A WALK."

9/16/69

11/17/69

1/8/70

"WANT SOME? WE GOT MILLIONS OF 'EM."

Vice-President Spiro Agnew left Honolulu December 27, 1969, on a 37,000-mile, 11-nation Asian tour. Before his return to Washington three weeks later, he pledged that the United States, already mired down in South Vietnam, wouldn't leave Southeast Asia "in the lurch."

"IT'S SPIRO AGNEW!"

12/15/69

4/29/70

82

"ZOOM, ROAR, ROAR, ZOOM!"

83

"I PRAISE THE LORD."   "I PASS THE AMMUNITION."   8/12/69

84

7/1/69

"SUPERB REFLEXES."

June 28, 1969: Nixon appointed Dr. Roger O. Egeberg as Assistant Secretary of Health, Education and Welfare for health and scientific affairs. The President's old friend HEW Secretary Robert Finch had wanted Dr. John H. Knowles, Director of Massachusetts General Hospital, for the post. Knowles, however, was a critic of rising medical costs and favored government-subsidized health programs. The AMA, through its political action committee (which contributed heavily to the Republican Party in 1968), was opposed to Knowles. His nomination was withdrawn.

"MEL, YOU'VE BEEN WORKING TOO HARD."   6/12/69

*Secretary of Defense Melvin Laird, the most recognizable
exponent of missiles on Capitol Hill.*

12/11/69

"DID YOU CHECK UNDER THE BED, JOHN?"

November 1969: Martha Mitchell, wife of Attorney General John Mitchell, called thousands of antiwar demonstrators who converged on Washington "very liberal Communists" and compared the peace moratoriums to the Russian Revolution. She also made it clear that she and her husband agree politically. Mitchell denied it, saying that his wife "doesn't understand the vernacular" and that "the dialogue got confused." Martha said she had misquoted herself.

11/26/69

"WE GOT COMPANY."

4/7/70

April 5, 1970: On the eve of the desegregation of the Manatee County school system, Florida Governor Claude Kirk personally assumed control of the county's board of public instruction and ordered pupils to ignore the integration plan ordered by Federal District Judge Ben Krentzman. For seven days he kept the system in confusion and controversy as he defied the court, suspended school board officials, petitioned for Supreme Court intervention and, according to U.S. District Attorney John Briggs, threatened to have state troopers fire on any U.S. marshal who attempted to arrest his aides. On April 11 he was found guilty of contempt of court and ordered to pay $10,000 per day for each day he continued to defy the order. On April 12, in a televised retreat, he agreed to reinstate the school board and order it to implement the plan.

WALLACE PLATFORM:

1. RUN OVER HIPPIES WITH YORE CAR.
2. WIN WAR—SOMEHOW.
3. THROW BUREAUCRATS BRIEFCASES IN POTOMAC.
4. RUN OVER YIPPIES WITH YORE CAR.
5. THROW BUREAUCRATS IN POTOMAC.
6. WAVE YORE FLAG.
7. PUT CROOKS IN JAIL.
8. PUT SUPREME COURT IN JAIL.
9. PUT PINK PRESS IN JAIL.
10. GET LAW AND ORDER.
11. GET A DIME'S WORTH OF DIFFERENCE.
12. DN
15. LET POLICE RUN COUNTRY

9/4/68

6/14/68

3/20/68

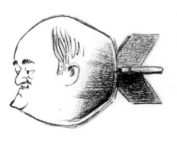

"MY HHH-BOMB"

4/29/68

As a presidential contender for 1968, Lyndon Baines John-son dropped out and unloaded Hubert on us.

12/5/70

*December 9, 1967: The last of Lady Bird's babies leaves the
nest. Lynda Bird married Marine Capt. Charles Robb.*

12/8/67

5/27/68

May 1968: The Republicans as they approached national convention time.

"THE TRICK IS NOT TO APPEAR OVERANXIOUS."   4/18/68

Some of Nelson Rockefeller couldn't make up his mind whether to run for President or not.

9/5/67

"A MR. ROMNEY TO SEE YOU."

Michigan's Governor George Romney personally inspected South Vietnam in 1965 and said he supported the Johnson Administration's war policy there. He made a second trip in 1967 as a possible Republican presidential contender and promptly observed that he had been "brainwashed" in 1965 and no longer supported the war. The remark hurt him politically. Nobody wanted a President whose brain could be washed that easily.

8/30/67

*August 29, 1967: Shirley Temple Black formally announced·
she was running for Congress as an Independent Republican
from California's 11th district on a ticket described at the
time as a "God, love and mother" effort. Dubbed "Lady
Hawk" by her opponents, she was very strong for the Vietnam war and demanded its conduct be turned over to the
Joint Chiefs of Staff.*

98

9/2/69

**"WHY, YES, SHIRLEY, THERE ARE COMMUNISTS
IN THE UNITED NATIONS."**

*August 29, 1969: Shirley sailed the good ship Lollipop back
into the limelight when she was appointed by President Nixon
as U.S. Representative to the United Nations, swearing to
defend the Constitution against all enemies, foreign and
domestic.*

8/15/64

August 1964: The Senate voted almost unanimously for the Gulf of Tonkin resolution which authorized President Johnson to take whatever measures he considered necessary against the North Vietnamese.

May 17, 1970: Angered by Nixon's invasion of Cambodia, Senate Majority Leader Mike Mansfield announced he would sponsor an amendment to cut off all funds for all U.S. military operations in Indochina by the end of the year. Prior to his announcement Congressional assault on White House authority to widen the war had already begun with the introduction of the Cooper–Church antiwar amendment. This amendment, attached to a foreign military sales bill, denied funds for retention of U.S. troops in Cambodia after July 1, forbade use of U.S. instructors, advisers or air power for the purpose of aiding the Cambodian government and barred U.S. financing of others to give such aid— unless first approved by the Congress.

5/19/70

THE ECONOMY

THE ECONOMY is not at all simple, even when simply administered. It involves budgets, inflation, depressions, unemployment, wage and price controls, cooling down, heating up, Federal spending, consumer protection, defense spending, interest rates, diddling the consumer, lying about defense spending, poverty spending, free enterprise, balance of payments, cutting back on poverty programs and having an ABM.

An ABM is an Anti-Ballistic-Missile system which some say might work and some say is a silly waste of money.

Nothing as complex as all that can be dealt with very thoroughly in cartoons. We really only scratch the surface, hoping to scrape some careless hides in the process.

9/26/69

September 23, 1969: Nixon said he would ask for $662 million over a five-year period to develop a supersonic transport aircraft capable of whizzing the well-to-do abroad at 1,800 miles per hour.

3/17/69

*March 14, 1969: Nixon announced that he had decided to
go ahead with a modified version of the Sentinel antiballistic
missile system.*

6/25/69

Secretary of Defense Melvin Laird presented the Administration's case for the ABM in testimony before the Senate Armed Services Committee. Laird insisted that, if properly interpreted by the Soviet Union, the ABM system would not trigger a new round of arms escalation. He also said it was the only way to prove to the Russians that America's strategic nuclear force was capable of full retaliation.

7/18/69

6/2/69

"—DRIVE THEIR ABM CRAZY"

Another of the Administration's strong arguments was that the ABM would protect us against the Soviet Union's known offensive capacity.

8/7/69

August 6, 1969: After months of controversy, the Senate narrowly approved the $7-billion ABM proposal. Critics of the system claimed it was tragically wasteful and probably ineffective.

5/20/70

Following Nixon's announcement of the U.S. invasion of Cambodia, the stock market went into an alarming tailspin. Analysts reported that the drop was due to a loss of confidence in the country's leadership.

5/28/69

PENTAGON

TAXPAYERS

3/25/69

"MAYBE IF YOU LEARNED TO KILL . . ."

6/12/67

9/23/69

"WATCH IT, FELLA—YOU'LL BEND MY CARTE BLANCHE CARD."

4/14/69

"H-H-HERBERT HOOVER!"

4/30/70

6/11/69

"HIT HIM AGAIN, HE'S STILL SPENDING!"

5/5/69

8/29/69

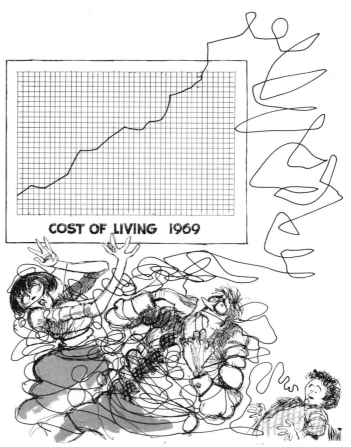

8/1/69

2/26/69

"BLACK CAPITALISM! AFTER ALL WE'VE DONE FOR YOU, BOY?"

SPRING FLOOD

5/28/69

2/11/69

AN ORIGINAL PAINTING BY RICHARD MILHOUS NIXON
ENTITLED "THE ECONOMY" WHICH, ACCORDING TO
THE ARTIST, DEPICTS THE SUN RISING OVER A LUSH,
GREEN VALLEY AS SPRITES PLAY FLUTES AND DANCE
MIDST DEW-KISSED GOLDEN BUTTERCUPS.

5/26/70

3/27/69   "COST OF LIVING WENT UP. GOOD THING WE AIN'T LIVING."

THE COURT, THE KOOKS

THOMAS JEFFERSON never got ecstatic over the Supreme Court. Andrew Jackson was disgusted with it most of the time and Abraham Lincoln got mad enough to ask for a reexamination of the high tribunal. Theodore Roosevelt tried to recall it and Franklin Roosevelt wanted it reorganized.

Lyndon Johnson and Richard Nixon have fared no better, suffering considerable embarrassment over appointments and decisions.

But few have attacked the Supreme Court with the consistent frenzy of the heaving, rabid right, so noisy and shrill with their simplicities and yet at times so hard to make out. Sometimes you can catch the glint of their crazy little eyes peering out of the darkness and hear their voices, as if in a tunnel, calling "Wake Up America!" and "Cancel my subscription!"

4/8/69

April 7, 1969: The U.S. Supreme Court ruled that obscenity in the home is legal. The justices, who agreed that the "state has no business telling a man sitting alone in his own home what books he may read or what films he may watch," said it cannot constitutionally be made a crime to possess obscene films or printed matter in the privacy of a man's home.

5/12/69

"FORTAS IS OVERCOMPENSATING."

May 14, 1969: In the midst of a raging controversy over his ethics and associations, Supreme Court Associate Justice Abe Fortas resigned his seat. In a private, four-page letter of resignation sent to his chief justice, Earl Warren, Fortas maintained his innocence and said that at no time had there been "any wrong doing on my part."

"GOOD MORNING, CHIEF BURGER."

5/23/69

May 21, 1969: Warren E. Burger was nominated by President Nixon as fifteenth chief justice of the Supreme Court. The law and order judge was confirmed by the Senate June 9 and sworn in June 23.

August 18, 1969: President Nixon nominated Clement F. Haynsworth, Jr., a 57-year-old South Carolina jurist, to the Supreme Court. Haynsworth, before being rejected on November 21, 1969, by a 55–45 vote in the Senate, was the subject of a national controversy over his qualifications, previous decisions, ethics and alleged conflicts of interest.

10/3/69

HERE COME DE JUDGE

Part of the conflict surrounding Haynsworth was his purchase of 1,000 shares of Brunswick Corporation stock after ruling for Brunswick in a case even before the decision was final and made public.

9/25/69

"—AND NOW, GENTLEMEN OF THE SENATE, THOSE OPPOSED TO HIRAM P. SUCKLESHEW FOR THE SUPREME COURT..."

4/9/70

April 8, 1970: In his second attempt to seat a Southern judge on the U.S. Supreme Court bench, Richard Nixon became the first President in this century—and only the fourth in the nation's history—to have more than one nominee rejected by the Senate. Florida Judge G. Harrold Carswell was defeated by a vote of 51 to 45.

6/24/69

"DOUGLAS!"

5/19/69

REASON FOR CAMPUS UNREST: COMMUNISM
REASON FOR RIOTS IN SLUMS: COMMUNISM
REASON FOR SLUMS: COMMUNISM
REASON FOR HIPPIES: COMMUNISM
REASON FOR POOR PEOPLE: COMMUNISM
REASON FOR DISSENT: COMMUNISM
REASON FOR DIRTY PICTURES: COMMUNISM
REASON FOR SMOKING POT: COMMUNISM
REASON FOR DIRTY MOVIES: COMMUNISM
REASON FOR A.C.L.U.: COMMUNISM
REASON FOR DIRTY BOOKS: COMMUNISM
REASON FOR BAD NEWS: COMMUNISM
REASON FOR L.S.D.: COMMUNISM
REASON FOR CATNIP: COMMUNISM
REASON FOR FLOURIDE: COMMUNISM
REASON FOR _____: COMMU
(FILL IN BLANK)

3/11/69

11/14/69

132

6/26/69

"DIRTY TALK ABOUT HAVING BABIES IS FOR PARENTS ONLY!" 5/15/69

3/18/69

"KIND OF BLOWS YOUR WHOLE ACT, DON'T IT?"

THE MOON

"WE CAN go to the moon but we can't clean up the ghettos."

"We can go to the moon but the toilet's stopped up."

Or, "We can go to the moon but Harold's got hemorrhoids."

Well, we went to the moon.

Even those who raised hell about how much it cost are damned proud of it.

7/21/69

July 20, 1969: Apollo 11 astronauts Neil Armstrong and Edwin Aldrin became the first men to set foot on the moon.

7/15/69

For a while it seemed as if four men would make the journey to the moon.

President Nixon, who telephoned the astronauts on the moon from his White House office, was not allowed to greet them personally on their return. He talked with them only after they were safely quarantined in a trailer aboard the recovery ship, the U.S.S. Hornet. The quarantine was an effort to protect earth life from alien elements or organisms they might have brought back.

7/25/69

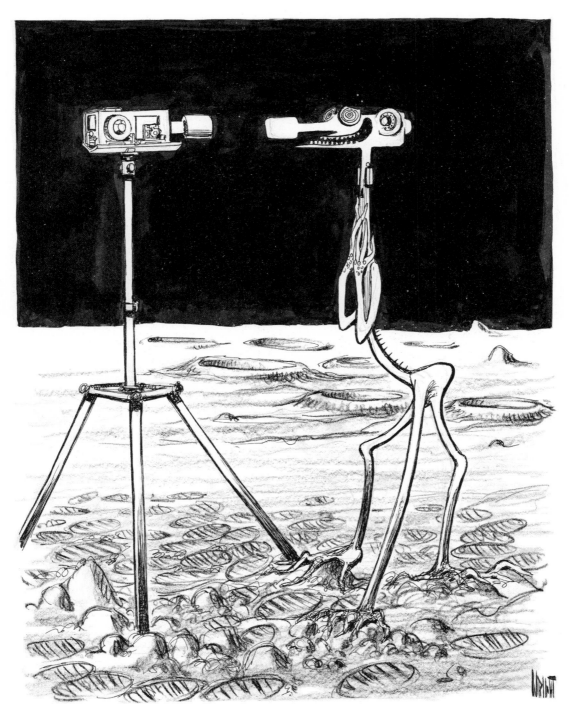

"WILL YOU MARRY ME?"

8/15/69

Apollo 11 astronauts left almost $1 million worth of cameras, tools and breathing equipment on the moon. That included the $250,000 black-and-white television camera which captured the moonwalk, a $50,000 Kodak and an $11,176 Hasselblad.

5/26/69

"THE PRESIDENT SAYS IGNORE THEM."   11/19/69

November 19, 1969: Apollo 12 lands on the moon, four days after the second moratorium and just over a month after the first massive peace demonstration at which time the President watched football on television and said he could not abandon his present policies in Vietnam "merely because of public demonstration."

4/15/70

On April 17, 1970, America's most dramatic space voyage came to an end when astronauts Jim Lovell, Fred Haise and John Swigert splashed down safely in the South Pacific. Their spacecraft, Apollo 13, had suffered an explosion on a flight to the moon and for 87 hours the men battled for survival, rationing water, oxygen and power in an effort to keep the crippled craft functioning long enough to bring them home.

– AND –

BITS and pieces that seem to defy categories...

"I THINK HE CHICKENED!"

12/31/69

6/9/69

"YOU COULD BE THE ABE FORTAS OF PRO FOOTBALL."

June 6, 1969: A month after Supreme Court Justice Abe Fortas resigned, Joe Namath, quarterback of the New York Jets, tearfully announced that he was quitting pro football rather than dispose of his financial interest in the Bachelors III, a Manhattan lounge, which football commissioner Pete Rozelle said was frequented by "undesirable characters."

January 6, 1969: Just prior to the big Superbowl game in New Orleans, Louisiana, stories broke about a federal probe of a nationwide sports gambling ring involving professional football players.

1/9/70

**"HAROLD DIDN'T GO TO WORK THIS MORNING.
I THINK HE'S PREGNANT."**

5/13/69

In 1969 women's rights was heralded as the "new movement of the next decade." President Nixon appointed a Presidential Task Force on Women's Rights and Responsibilities and the National Organization for Women called for an Equal Rights Constitutional Amendment.

5/4/70

"NOW WIGGLE THOSE LITTLE OLD BUNNY EARS, HEFNER."

8/1/68

5/6/69 **"I HEAR OLD BANANA NOSE IS GONE."**

April 28, 1969: French President Charles de Gaulle resigned after being repudiated in a national referendum. It ended an epoch in French history and for the first time provided an opportunity for Great Britain to enter the European Common Market—a move de Gaulle had opposed.

November 22, 1967: The House of Commons gave British Prime Minister Harold Wilson a parliamentary green light for devaluation of the ailing pound sterling and a tough new dose of economic belt tightening for all Britons. The endorsement came at about the same time another Briton was also making the lean look fashionable—Twiggy, a 17-year-old model who weighed 92 pounds and measured 31–23–32.

TWIGGY 11/23/67

11/21/69   "WELL, WE DON'T HAVE NIXON TO KICK AROUND ANYMORE."

In 1962, after Richard M. Nixon was defeated in his attempt to become governor of California, he angrily assailed the press, telling them they wouldn't have the old Nixon to kick around anymore. On November 13, 1969, President Richard M. Nixon's vice-president, Spiro Agnew, assaulted the press for its biased television news reporting and unprecedented concentration of power over public opinion and suggested that perhaps the time had come to make the media "more responsive to the views of the nation."

"AND YOU KNOW WHAT ELSE I NOTICED ABOUT THE PRESIDENT, ROG? ONE HECKUVVA SWEET SMILE."

12/10/69

Part of the Vice-President's criticism at the Midwest regional Republican committee meeting in Des Moines, Iowa, was the "instant analysis and querulous criticism" of commentators who followed Nixon's November 3 Vietnam speech.

152

7/28/69

July 22, 1969: The Spanish Parliament promptly ratified Generalissimo Francisco Franco's nomination of thirty-one-year-old Prince Juan Carlos of Bourbon as successor designate to the throne of Spain.

4/28/70

April 24, 1970: An official communiqué transmitted in Hong Kong by the New China News Agency announced that the Red Chinese had launched their first satellite. It weighed 381 pounds, circled the globe every 114 minutes and broadcast a Chinese revolutionary song entitled "The East is Red." Accentuating the ideological aspect of the launching is this couplet from the song:

> *The East is Red. The*
> *Sun Rises*
> *Mao Tse-tung emerges*
> *in the East.*

7/3/68

"HAVANA? WHAT THE HELL'S HAVANA?" 12/5/68

INTEROFFICE

THE FOLLOWING are rough sketches—drawn over a period of time on a variety of topics—tossed on the editor's desk, not necessarily for publication but just for the pure pleasure of watching his face react to inspiration gone maverick.

"FOR CHRIST'S SAKE, KNOCK IT OFF!"

2/69

3/70

11/69

"I READ YOUR HARD-HITTING AND INCISIVE EDITORIAL ON THE RESPONSIBILITY OF TODAY'S PRESS IN WHICH YOU READILY ADMIT THAT NEWSPAPERS ARE GUILTY OF SUCH THINGS AS SENSATIONALISM, INABILITY TO RELATE TO THE MASSES, FAULTY REPORTING, LACK OF IMAGINATION, MONOPOLIES AND INEPT LEADERSHIP. NOW GO BACK AND WRITE SOMETHING WE CAN USE."

1/68

10/68

"I WONDER WHAT ARISTOTLE IS DOING NOW."

—collision at sea, the Pueblo incident and even a submarine that, when christened, slid down the ramp and sank. The Navy couldn't seem to get it all together.

159

11/69

"WALTER CRONKITE"

3/70

12/69

7/69

JESUS IS
COMING
GET READY

7/69

7/69

5/69

**"THE GIRLS AND I WOULD LOVE TO HEAR
YOU SAY 'SONOFABITCH.' "**

**"GET YOUR ASS OUT TO THE YOUTH
FOR DECENCY RALLY!"**

3